D0575256

GREAT MINDS OF SCIENCE

Louis Pasteur

Disease Fighter

Linda Wasmer Smith

 Enslow Publishers, Inc.

44 Fadem Road	PO Box 38
Box 699	Aldershot
Springfield, NJ 07081	Hants GU12 6BP
USA	UK

Library of Congress Cataloging-in-Publication Data

Smith, Linda Wasmer
    Louis Pasteur: disease fighter / Linda W. Smith
      p. cm. — (Great minds of science)
    Includes bibliographical references and index.
    Summary: A biography of the noted French scientist whose discoveries,
including a rabies vaccine and the process of pasteurization, had
important practical applications in both medicine and industry.
    ISBN 0-89490-790-5
    1. Pasteur, Louis, 1822–1895—Biography—Juvenile literature. 2. Milk—
Pasteurization—History—Juvenile literature. 3. Rabies vaccines—
History—Juvenile literature. 4. Scientists—France—Biography—Juvenile
literature. 5. Microbiologists—France—Biography—Juvenile literature.
[1. Pasteur, Louis, 1822–1895. 2. Scientists.] I. Title. II. Series.
Q143.P2S55 1997
509'.2—dc21
  [B]   96-38082
                                        CIP
                                        AC

Printed in the United States of America

10 9 8 7 6 5 4 3 2 1

Illustration Credits: Barry-Wehmiller Company, St. Louis, Mo., p. 53;
The Burndy Library, Dibner Institute for the History of Science and
Technology, pp. 10, 25, 45, 68, 86, 88, 106; The French Government
Tourist Office, pp. 13, 15; National Library of Medicine, Bethesda,
Md., pp. 9, 22, 33, 40, 60, 75, 81, 83, 91, 95, 97, 98, 102; U. S.
Department of Agriculture, p. 51.

Cover Credit: National Library of Medicine, Bethesda, Md.; Visuals
Unlimited/Tim Hauf.

Contents

A Hero Is Born

THE CHRISTMAS OF 1822 MUST HAVE been a joyous one for the Pasteur family. A new baby was on the way. The parents' first child, a son, had died while still a baby. Their second child, a daughter named Virginie, had been born in 1818. Now a third child was about to be born.

The family lived in Dôle, a small town in eastern France. The father, Jean-Joseph Pasteur, was a tanner, a person who makes animal hides into leather. Jean-Joseph's own father had also been a tanner. You might think that he would want his child to grow up to be a tanner, too, but Jean-Joseph had bigger dreams.

As a young man, Jean-Joseph had seen something of the wider world. He had fought as a soldier in the army of the emperor of France, Napoleon I, one of the greatest military geniuses of his time. Napoleon built an empire that covered most of western and central Europe. That empire collapsed in 1814. But Jean-Joseph never forgot those days of glory, when France seemed to be on top of the world.[1]

From that time on, Jean-Joseph spent many nights reading history books. He tried to teach himself about history and science, and he hoped one day to have a son who would become a teacher in the local school.[2]

In 1816, Jean-Joseph had married Jeanne Roqui, the daughter of a gardener. Jeanne was a lively person, a good match for her quiet husband. The couple lived in the same small building that held Jean-Joseph's tannery, and Jeanne worked hard to make this humble home a happy one.

On December 27, 1822, Jean-Joseph and Jeanne's third child was born. The baby was a boy, and they named him Louis. Here at last was the son they had so wanted. Louis would, in fact, grow up to be a professor. He would also become one of the greatest scientists of his day and a founder of modern medicine.

Louis Pasteur's discoveries about the way germs spread disease would help save countless lives. Germs are simple living things, too small to be seen without a microscope, that can cause disease. Another word for germ is "microbe."

Pasteur would also be remembered as the inventor of pasteurization. This is a process for heating milk or other liquids hot enough and long enough to kill harmful microbes called bacteria. Bacteria are very tiny and simple living things. Some bacteria cause disease, but others do helpful things, such as turning cider into vinegar.

In addition, Pasteur developed the rabies vaccine. Rabies is a disease that people can get from the bite of an infected animal. A vaccine is a preparation of weakened or killed microbes that is given to people to prevent a disease. The vaccine tells the body to be prepared to fight the rabies microbe the next time it is found. Unless rabies is prevented in this way, it almost always leads to death.

Of course, there were other great scientists who lived at the same time as Pasteur. Few were as honored, however. That's because Pasteur was thought of not only as a genius but also as a hero. It was said that he devoted his own life to making life better for all people. In fact, the British scientist Stephen Paget once called him "the most perfect man who has ever entered the Kingdom of Science."[3]

Louis Pasteur was without doubt a remarkable man, but he wasn't perfect. Like anyone else, he had his flaws. One may have been a lack of total honesty. When Pasteur was fifty-five, he told his family never to show anyone his private lab notebooks. For many years, they did as he wished. It was not until Pasteur's grandson died

Louis Pasteur, the inventor of pasteurization and the rabies vaccine.
He made major contributions to chemistry, biology, and medicine.

in 1971 that most scientists had a chance to see what Louis Pasteur had written there.

These notebooks were records of experiments that Pasteur had done. It turns out that he did not always do his experiments exactly the way he claimed. In a few cases, he may have altered his results to make his work look better.[4]

A sample of Pasteur's cramped, messy handwriting. Pasteur kept lengthy notes, which tell us about his experiments and ideas.

Yet these notebooks show the best side of Pasteur, too. Page after page, the 102 notebooks record a lifetime of hard, careful work. For forty years, Pasteur and his helpers spent almost every day on his research. There are perhaps ten thousand pages in all that are filled with Pasteur's hard-to-read handwriting.

Pasteur made not just one, but several big discoveries in his career. This led some people to say that he was lucky. Pasteur himself said that "chance favors only the prepared mind."[5] In other words, luck only helps those who are ready to recognize it. Pasteur was surely a bright and hardworking man, yet his greatest gift may have been his ability to notice the little things that other people missed. Some of those little things proved to be his lucky breaks.

Life at the Tannery

LOUIS AND HIS FAMILY MOVED TWO TIMES before he was five. First they moved in 1825 to the nearby town of Marnoz, the native village of his mother's family. Then they moved to the neighboring town of Arbois in 1827.

Arbois sits at the foot of the Jura Mountains in eastern France. The town is surrounded by lovely meadows and vineyards, fields planted with grapevines. Louis's family soon came to love the place. This is where Louis grew up. And even after he was famous, this is where he spent his summers.

By the time the Pasteurs settled in Arbois,

there were two more members of the family. In addition to his older sister, Virginie, Louis had two younger sisters. Josephine was born while the family lived in Dôle. Emilie was born in Marnoz.

The four Pasteur children and their parents shared a small house at Arbois. They lived above the tanning tubs there. This house is now a

A room from the Pasteur home in Arbois. Today the home has been turned into a museum.

museum. Visitors today can see Louis's school prizes and science books, among other things.[1]

In 1829, Louis began school in Arbois. As a young boy, he was just an average student. He showed no early signs of scientific genius. It was not until he was a teenager that Louis started winning many prizes for his schoolwork.

In fact, Louis's main talent as a boy seemed to be a knack for art. Many of his pastel drawings of friends and family have been saved. They show that young Louis had a good eye for detail. In one portrait of his mother, she wears a white bonnet and a blue-and-green-checkered shawl. Her face has a calm but determined look. This seems to be what Louis's mother was really like, both in looks and in character.[2]

There is an interesting fact about Louis's drawings: The people in them are never smiling. They are always solemn and formal. This is not unlike Louis himself. Even as a child, Louis was serious and dutiful. And as an adult, he usually looked as serious as he probably felt. Only one known picture shows Louis smiling.[3]

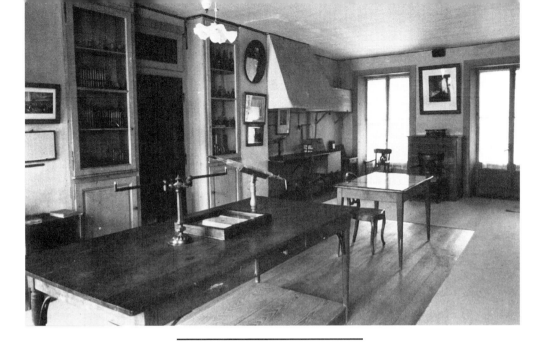

The lab at the Pasteur home in Arbois, where Louis Pasteur worked during summer visits as an adult.

Yet Louis sometimes liked to have fun, too. Arbois lies on the Cuisance River. Louis liked to fish there when he was a boy. He and his friends would follow the river upstream to a spot that was known for its fine trout fishing.

When Louis was eight, something happened that stuck in his mind for the rest of his life. A wolf with rabies wandered out of the woods of the Jura Mountains. It attacked and bit several people around Arbois. At the time, such bites were usually treated by burning them with a red-hot iron. No one was sure why burning the bites stopped many people from getting rabies. But the treatment didn't always work. Some people who had their bites burned this way still became sick from rabies and died.

Many of this wolf's victims came to the village blacksmith to have their wounds burned. The blacksmith shop in Arbois was located near the Pasteur home. Louis watched the scene in horror. From where he stood, he could hear the victims' screams of pain. Louis remembered this experience as an adult. It may be one reason he was later driven to try to find a way to prevent rabies.[4]

As Louis got older, he became a better student. When he was fifteen, he won a number of prizes at his school in Arbois. The headmaster urged him to prepare to take the entrance exam for the École Normale Supérieure in Paris. This is a college that trains people to become professors of the sciences or arts. Only a handful of students with top exam scores were admitted to the École Normale.

Louis's father decided to send him away to boarding school. This was difficult for a tanner to afford, but he thought that his son would get

*Pasteur grew up in eastern France, near the border with Switzerland.
In 1871, France lost Alsace-Lorraine, the region around Strasbourg,
in a war with Prussia.*

the preparation he needed there. So in October 1838, Louis and his friend Jules Vercel traveled to Paris. Louis was going to attend a boarding school run by a man named Barbet.

Louis and Jules set off on their long journey in a stagecoach. It was a wet and dreary morning when they left. As the church steeple of Arbois faded from view, Louis felt his heart sink. Nothing had prepared him for life in Paris, one of the world's busiest cities. As a village boy, he was simply not ready for the crowded buildings and noisy streets. Soon Louis was feeling deeply homesick.[5]

Barbet was so worried by Louis's sadness that he wrote to Louis's parents. In November 1838, Louis's father brought him home to Arbois. How did Louis feel about his failure to adjust to Paris? He may have been a bit ashamed, but that just made him work all the harder. Back at school in Arbois, he once again excelled. In fact, he won so many prizes at year's end that he couldn't carry them all. It seems that Louis was more determined than ever to make a success of his life.

The Call of Science

LOUIS HAD NOT GIVEN UP HIS DREAM OF studying at the École Normale. He decided to try preparatory school again. In 1839, he began attending the Royal College of Besançon. The town of Besançon is only about twenty-five miles from Arbois. Louis's father went there every month to sell leather goods from his tannery.

Perhaps the regular visits from his father helped, for this time Louis overcame his home-sickness. He did quite well in his classes at the college. In addition, Louis still liked to draw and paint. After one of his portraits was shown in the parlor of the college, he became known around town as "the artist."[1]

Louis enjoyed the praise he received for his artwork. Yet he knew it would not get him into the École Normale.[2] So Louis began to aim his attention in a new direction. In 1840, he took the exam for his Bachelor of Letters degree. He passed with "fair" marks in history and geography and "good" marks in Greek, Latin, language, and philosophy. But his only "excellent" mark came in basic science.

Louis was now determined to study science at the École Normale. But to do that, he first had to have a Bachelor of Science degree. To prepare for this second degree, he decided to stay at the Royal College of Besançon.

In his second year at the college, Louis was offered a job as an assistant teacher. In return for his work, he was given a room, meals, and a small salary. Although he was only eighteen, Louis was very busy as both a teacher and a student.

Louis passed the exam for his Bachelor of

Science degree in 1842. Days later, he passed the entrance exam for the École Normale.

Then something unexpected happened: Louis turned down the École Normale's offer of admission. Louis had ranked fifteenth on the entrance exam, but he felt that he could do better than that. So he decided to spend another year preparing. He would try the École Normale test again the next year. Even at this young age, Louis always strove for perfection. This is a trait he would show his whole life.

Paris was the center of learning in France. Louis knew that he had to return there. So at age nineteen, he headed back to Barbet's boarding school. This time, though, Louis was ready for the city. He helped teach the younger students, and he took classes at the Lycée Saint-Louis, a leading preparatory school.

At year's end, Louis received first prize in physics, the branch of science that deals with matter and energy. When he took the École Normale exam again, he ranked fourth. It was finally time for Louis to fulfill his dream.

Offert par Mr Deschiens.

Pasteur as he usually appeared in pictures: with a serious look.

In October 1843, Louis entered the École Normale. There he would study physics and chemistry, the science that deals with the different kinds of simple matter called chemical elements. One day, he would be a professor.

Students at the École Normale spent many hours in classes. In addition, they spent an hour each day using what they had learned. During this time, they might blow glass or build machines or make locks and keys. Louis worked hard at his lessons, so hard that his father worried about his health. But Louis was happy. Not only was he on the road to a career that would bring good pay and much respect; he had also started on the way to making his mark in science.[3]

A high point of Louis's student days in Paris was going to the lectures of Jean-Baptiste Dumas. This man was one of the greatest chemists of his day. He was also a powerful speaker. Louis was deeply impressed.[4] Dumas gave his lectures dressed in official-looking black. Large crowds came to hear him speak. His talks were clear and interesting, and his demonstrations were flawless.

Dumas sparked Louis's desire to know more about chemistry. Now Louis's favorite way to pass free time was working in the lab or taking a private lesson from Dumas's assistant. This love of science would last a lifetime.

Louis had yet another exam to take before becoming a professor. A good result on this qualifying exam for professors would open doors to the best jobs. Louis took the exam in 1846 and placed third in physical science. The men giving the test were impressed by his efforts. "He will make an excellent professor," they wrote.[5]

However, Louis was already heading down a different path. A month after the qualifying exam, Louis was offered a job as an assistant in chemistry. He would help the famous chemist Antoine-Jérôme Balard.

Twenty years earlier, Balard had discovered the chemical element called bromine. In later years, though, he was known not only for that accomplishment, but also for his simple living

Jean-Baptiste Dumas, the chemist who inspired Pasteur.

habits. It was said that when Balard traveled he took with him only a shirt and socks, wrapped in newspaper and carried in a pocket.

Not surprisingly, Balard's lab was simple, too. He even liked to make his students build their own equipment. Yet there Louis could do the research that would lead to a more advanced Doctor of Science degree. It was also in this lab that Louis would make the first of many important discoveries.

Gazing at Crystals

LOUIS PASTEUR WAS READY TO BEGIN his own research. He chose to study crystals, the regularly shaped objects that many substances form when they harden. Crystals have both sharp edges and flat surfaces. Think of pictures you've seen of a snowflake. Snow is nothing more than water vapor that has frozen into crystals.

Now imagine the lacy shape of a snowflake. It's easy to see why the artist in Pasteur would be drawn to the beauty of crystal shapes. There was also another reason crystals interested

Pasteur: There was a mystery about them, and Pasteur was determined to solve it.

It was already known that some crystals bend light that passes through them. This property is called optical activity. It was also known that some crystals turn light to the right, while others turn it to the left. This seemed to be related to the shape of the crystal. Some crystals were shaped in a "right-handed" way and bent light to the right, while others were "left-handed" and bent light to the left.

Pasteur focused on two kinds of crystals that formed in the vats where wine was made. They are called tartaric acid and racemic acid. There was something strange about these crystals; they seemed to have the same crystal shape, but while the tartaric acid was optically active, the racemic acid was not.

Pasteur thought that there had to be something different about the two types of crystals. He was sure that this difference had just never before been noticed. He was determined to find out what it was.

Pasteur began his work with crystals in 1847. He completed his Doctor of Science degree in August of that year, but his interest in crystals continued. Pasteur spent many hours bent over his lab bench. He peered tirelessly through a microscope at crystals. He used his artist's skill to draw what he saw there. He also built special instruments for measuring the way the crystals bent the light.

Then something exciting happened. One day in April 1848, Pasteur looked up from his lab bench and exclaimed, "I have it!"[1] What he had found were tiny surface pieces called facets. In the tartaric acid, all of the facets pointed in the same direction. But in the racemic acid, some facets pointed one way, while others pointed in the opposite direction. No one had noticed these facets before.

Pasteur hypothesized that some of the racemic acid facets bent light to the right and others to the left. The two kinds of facets combined canceled each other out, which explained why racemic acid was not optically active. When

Pasteur tested this idea in the lab, the results were just as he had predicted.

Pasteur was so thrilled by his findings that he rushed from the lab. He grabbed a lab assistant and said, "I have just made a great discovery."[2] Then he led the man into the garden and told him about what he had found.

Pasteur was only twenty-five years old at the time. News of the young man's remarkable discovery soon spread throughout Paris. It reached French scientist Jean-Baptiste Biot, who had earlier done important work on optical activity. Biot had Pasteur repeat the experiment for him. When he saw the results, Biot exclaimed, "My dear son, I have loved science so deeply that this stirs my heart."[3]

This was Pasteur's first big contribution to science. His work formed the basis of stereochemistry, a new branch of chemistry. Stereochemistry deals with the position in space of tiny particles called atoms and how this affects such things as optical activity.

At about the same time, there was much

excitement outside the walls of the École Normale. The French king was unpopular. A revolution had broken out, and Paris was in an uproar. Pasteur even joined the National Guard, a citizen army. Then in May 1848, his mother died. Pasteur blamed her death partly on her worries about his safety. He decided that it would be best if he left Paris.

That fall, Pasteur moved to the French city of Dijon. He worked as a physics professor at a local school there, but he hoped to get a better teaching job soon.[4] That wish came true within just a few weeks.

In January 1849, Pasteur became a professor of chemistry at the University of Strasbourg. The city of Strasbourg is in northeastern France. Pasteur continued his studies on crystals at the university in addition to teaching. During his five years at Strasbourg, Pasteur received the first major honors of his career. In 1853, for example, he was given the Legion of Honor medal.

However, the most important change in

Pasteur's life at this time had nothing to do with work. Soon after coming to Strasbourg, Pasteur met the daughter of a university official. Her name was Marie Laurent.

Marie was twenty-two years old at the time. She was a gentle young woman with clear blue eyes. For Pasteur, it was love at first sight. The custom of the day was to ask a woman's parents for permission to marry her. In February 1849, Pasteur wrote a letter to Marie's father. He was frank about his situation. He wrote, "My only assets are good health, an honest heart, and my position at the university."[5]

Marie's father must have felt that was quite enough. Louis Pasteur and Marie Laurent were married in Strasbourg on May 29, 1849. The story goes that Pasteur spent the morning of the wedding working in his lab. He became so wrapped up in what he was doing there that he had to be reminded to go to the church.[6]

Louis and Marie Pasteur's marriage lasted forty-six years, until Pasteur's death in 1895. By all accounts, it was a splendid match. Marie

Pasteur understood her husband's devotion to science. She helped with his work and accepted his odd habits.

On their thirty-fifth wedding anniversary, Marie Pasteur wrote to her daughter: "Your father, very busy as always, says little to me, sleeps little, and gets up at dawn."[7] Not every

Jean-Baptiste Biot, the scientist for whom Pasteur named his son.

woman could have been satisfied with such a marriage, but the Pasteurs seem to have been very happy together.

The Pasteurs' first three children were born while they still lived in Strasbourg. Their oldest child, a daughter named Jeanne, was born in 1850. Their son, Jean-Baptiste, was born the following year. He was named after Jean-Baptiste Biot. Another daughter, Cécile, came in 1853. Two more daughters followed in later years: Marie-Louise, born in 1858, and Camille, born in 1863.

The Strasbourg years were an exciting time for the Pasteur family, but they were just the start of Pasteur's long and fruitful career. Pasteur himself seemed to sense this. He wrote to a friend that his wife sometimes scolded him for working so hard. "I console her," he wrote, "by telling her that I will lead her to posterity."[8]

The Beet Juice Problem

THE YEAR 1854 FOUND PASTEUR READY for another change. He took a new job as professor of chemistry and dean of sciences at the University of Lille. The city of Lille, in northern France, is a center of industry. It was understood that Pasteur would focus his teaching and research on the practical needs of the region.

Then, as now, some scientists felt that they should care only about pure science. They were concerned only with theories, explanations based on observation and reasoning. However, Pasteur also believed in the value of applied science. He thought it was part of a scientist's job to put ideas to practical use.

One day in 1856, a man named Bigo asked Pasteur for help. Bigo owned a local factory where alcohol was made, in this case from beet juice. Alcohol is a colorless liquid used in manufacturing and medicine. The production of alcohol was a major industry in Lille. Bigo was having problems with flaws in his alcohol. He turned to Pasteur, who was his son's professor, for advice.

Alcohol is produced from beet juice by a process known as fermentation. This is a gradual chemical change in which sugar is changed into alcohol and carbon dioxide gas. Sugar is found in foods such as beets. It is also found in grapes, which naturally turn into wine as a result of fermentation. Thus, fermentation is the source of the alcohol found in alcoholic beverages.

Pasteur became a frequent visitor to Bigo's factory. He took some of the fermenting juice back to his lab. He looked at the juice under the microscope there. Then he wrote descriptions and made drawings of what he saw. This was one of the things that prompted Pasteur to study fermentation. He grew fascinated with the subject. It became the center of his research for several years.

At the time, people already knew that yeast had a role in fermentation. We now know that yeast is made up of tiny, one-celled living things that grow quickly in the presence of sugar. You may be familiar with a common use for yeast: It is what makes bread dough rise. The carbon dioxide bubbles produced during fermentation are what cause the dough to swell.

Back in the 1830s, the German scientist Theodor Schwann proposed that fermentation was due to living yeast cells. Schwann was not believed by most scientists of his day, however. Most people in the 1850s still thought that fermentation was a purely chemical process. As a chemist, Pasteur might have been expected to share this strictly chemical view, but his careful observations with the microscope had convinced him that fermentation was rooted in life. He set out to prove this.

In August 1857, Pasteur presented a famous paper. It dealt with lactic acid fermentation. This is the kind of fermentation that occurs when lactose, the sugar in milk, is changed into lactic acid. This is what happens when milk goes sour.

The paper laid out two revolutionary ideas: First, it said that microorganisms cause fermentation. Microorganisms are simple living things too small to be seen without a microscope. Yeast and bacteria are examples of microorganisms. Second, it said that specific kinds of microorganisms cause specific types of fermentation. For example, yeast is the microorganism that produces alcoholic fermentation. Another kind of microorganism would produce a different kind of change.

Now the things that Pasteur had seen in Bigo's beet juice made more sense. Some of the tiny objects he had viewed under the microscope were living yeast cells, needed to change sugar into alcohol. However, other tiny objects he had seen there were different microorganisms that were causing unwanted changes. They were the reason Bigo was having trouble making good alcohol.

Pasteur's 1857 paper is still considered a landmark in science. It introduced what is called the germ theory of fermentation. Later he would help develop the even more important germ theory of disease. Today Pasteur is known as a founder of microbiology, the branch of science that deals with microorganisms.

Once again, a major discovery meant a major change for Pasteur. In October 1857, he became director of scientific studies at the École Normale, his old school. This was an important job, but it didn't provide a lab. So Pasteur's first task upon returning to Paris was to find a place to carry out his research.

Pasteur soon found two unused rooms in an attic. The roof was so low there that he was unable to stand up straight. Yet Pasteur set about turning these rooms into a lab. A couple of years later, he moved his lab into a building with five

An enlarged lab at the École Normale, where Pasteur worked in later years. This famous portrait was painted by Paul Edelfelt.

small rooms on two floors. Even there, space was quite limited. In fact, he kept some of his equipment under a staircase. The only way to reach it was by crawling.

Pasteur was also short on money. In 1859, he wrote to the Minister of Public Education: "I have absolutely no means to meet the everyday expenses of my research work."[1] This was a worry for many years to come.

Despite these problems, Pasteur made great progress. He continued to learn about fermentation and the microorganisms that cause it.

Then tragedy struck the Pasteur family. The Pasteurs' oldest child, nine-year-old Jeanne, was visiting her grandfather in Arbois. She became ill with typhoid fever, a disease that causes a high fever and attacks the intestines.

Today we know that pure water, pasteurized milk, and clean food handling are the best ways to prevent typhoid fever. In addition, a vaccine offers partial protection against the disease. Doctors today also know how to treat typhoid fever with antibiotic drugs, which work against diseases caused by bacteria and certain other microorganisms. In earlier days, though, people didn't know how to prevent or treat typhoid fever, and it was often fatal. Jeanne died in September 1859. Her father was heartbroken by her death.

Nothing could keep Pasteur from his work for long, however. The very next year marked the start of a new direction in his research. It was a crucial turning point—not only in Pasteur's life, but in the history of science.

The Swan-necked Flask

IN THE PARIS OF 1860, A DEBATE RAGED in scientific circles. People were talking about a book published the year before by Félix-Archiméde Pouchet. The book dealt with spontaneous generation, the theory that living things can arise from nonliving matter. Pouchet claimed that the theory was correct.

Many people disagreed, of course. But the other side needed a strong voice. The Academy of Sciences offered a cash prize to the scientist who could produce the best proof for or against spontaneous generation.

Pasteur wanted to see the issue settled once

and for all.[1] He also needed the money. So he entered the debate, despite the fact that he was still new to biology, the science that deals with living things. A series of clever experiments followed. By the time Pasteur was finished, he had won the 2,500-franc prize. More importantly, he had shown beyond a doubt that the theory of spontaneous generation was false.

In a famous set of experiments, Pasteur put liquid into several flasks, which are glass bottles. Then he boiled the liquid and drove the air out of the flasks to get rid of any old microorganisms already there. Finally he sealed the flasks to keep the contents pure. Pasteur took the flasks to different spots, where he opened them briefly. He let the outside air, which carried new microorganisms, touch the liquid inside. Then he resealed the flasks and took them back to his lab for observation.

Pasteur waited and watched to see what would grow in the formerly pure liquid. This would show which microorganisms the surrounding air had held. He found that when the flasks were opened in dusty streets and cellars, the liquid was soon cloudy with microorganisms. But he still needed to show that it was microorganisms in the air, and not just air itself, that gave rise to this life.

Pasteur hypothesized that the cleaner the air, the fewer the microorganisms it would carry. To test this, he went to his childhood home of

One of Pasteur's microscopes. Pasteur would use microscopes to examine microbes and disprove the theory of spontaneous generation.

Arbois. He opened twenty flasks in the countryside there. Then he strapped another twenty flasks on a mule's back and climbed to an icy mountain peak. There he opened the flasks to the cold, fresh wind. Microorganisms later grew in eight of the samples from the country, but they grew in only one of the samples from the mountain with its nearly germ-free air.

Pasteur used swan-necked flasks for some of his experiments. The glass necks of these flasks were shaped like a long "S." They did indeed look like the graceful necks of swans. Pasteur's old chemistry professor, Antoine-Jérôme Balard, had suggested the novel shape. The liquid inside these flasks was boiled to make it pure, but even though the flasks were then left unsealed, no microorganisms grew inside.

Air was getting into the open flasks. However, Pasteur argued that microorganisms in the air were becoming trapped in the bend of the flask necks. That was why the liquid stayed pure. To prove his point, Pasteur tilted the flasks so that the liquid poured into the neck bends. Microorganisms soon appeared.

The debate over spontaneous generation came to a head in 1864. On April 7, Pasteur gave a lecture on the subject at the Sorbonne University in Paris. Scientists, writers, and even a princess came to hear him speak. They were expecting a great performance. Pasteur did not disappoint them. He showed the audience one of his swan-necked flasks. He told them, "Never will the doctrine of spontaneous generation recover from the mortal blow of this simple experiment."[2]

At the same time, Pasteur was also working on other problems. He was still studying fermentation in his lab.

One day, he was looking through a microscope at a drop of sugary liquid that was fermenting. At first, all the bacteria in the drop were very active, but soon Pasteur noticed something odd: The bacteria around the edge of the drop had stopped moving, while those in the center of the drop still moved. He guessed that air—or more precisely, the oxygen in air—was bad for these bacteria. It turned out to be a shrewd guess. Pasteur was the first scientist to realize that some bacteria are only active when no oxygen is present. He called these bacteria anaerobic, from the Greek for "without air."

Pasteur was very busy throughout this time. In addition to his work at the École Normale, he began teaching science at the École des Beaux-Arts in Paris. This was a school of fine arts. He taught about the chemistry of paints and the way building design affects health and comfort.

By 1863, Pasteur had made a name for himself as a brilliant scientist. Word of his accomplishments had even reached Emperor Napoleon III. The emperor asked to meet with Pasteur at the royal palace in Paris.

What a thrill this must have been for the forty-year-old scientist! He had been raised on stories of French glory. Now he was talking to the emperor himself. During their meeting, the emperor asked Pasteur to study the problems of wine-making. Pasteur agreed, and he didn't forget his promise.

From Grapes to Wine

IN PASTEUR'S DAY, AS NOW, FRANCE WAS famous for its wines. Since Pasteur had grown up near vineyards, he was well aware of this. He had not forgotten his goal of helping French industries. So perhaps it was natural that he would one day turn his knowledge of fermentation to helping the winemakers.

Wine is made from fermented grapes. The process, however, was as much an art as a science. Sometimes everything would go just right, and the taste would be perfect. Other times, though, something would go wrong. The wine would end up bitter or sour. Pasteur hoped to find out how to prevent such problems.

Pasteur remembered what he had seen in the beet juice from Bigo's factory. Other microorganisms, besides just yeast, were present when the alcohol went bad. He guessed that this was also true when the wine soured.

In addition, Pasteur knew that vinegar was made from alcohol created by fermentation. Vinegar has a very sour taste. Pasteur thought the same bacteria that produce vinegar might be making the wine go sour.

To test his theory, Pasteur turned to his childhood friends in Arbois. He set up a makeshift lab for the study of wine in an old café there. Since the café sign was left in the window, people sometimes came by looking for food. They usually stopped at the door after seeing the strange-looking equipment inside.

Pasteur studied many samples of wine under his microscope. He found that his theory was correct. There were many problems that could affect a wine's taste. And most could be traced to a particular microorganism. For example, *Mycoderma aceti* is the kind of bacteria that is involved in the production of vinegar. As Pasteur suspected, this type of bacteria can also make wine go sour.

The next step was to rid the wine of these unwanted microorganisms. In 1865, Pasteur

Pasteurization in the 1920s. The pasteurized milk flows over refrigeration pipes into bottling and capping machines.

began treating wine with heat. He found that he could kill off harmful bacteria by heating wine for several minutes to 55°C (131°F). The process didn't change the wine's taste, and wine treated this way could be stored indefinitely.

Sterilization is the act of making something free of microorganisms. The process of heating a liquid hot enough and long enough to kill harmful bacteria is called partial sterilization. However, this process soon became known as pasteurization, in honor of its developer. Pasteur took an interest in designing equipment that could heat large amounts of liquid at low cost. His writings on wine, vinegar, and beer have drawings of such equipment.

It was soon shown that pasteurization could be used for a wide range of drinks and foods. Among them are wine, vinegar, beer, juice, milk, cheese, and eggs. Nearly all of the milk sold in the United States today is pasteurized. This is usually done by heating the milk to 72°C (161.6°F) for fifteen seconds. The healthful vitamins and minerals in milk aren't harmed by

Pasteurization in the 1990s. This type of pasteurizer can be used for juices, fruit drinks, salsa, soy sauce, and pickles.

this process. It just lets the milk keep longer before going sour. It also prevents some diseases that are caused by bacteria found in untreated milk.[1]

"Pasteurization" is now a familiar word around the world. It is one way Pasteur's name lives on more than a hundred years after his death.

Saving the Silkworms

WINE-MAKING WASN'T THE ONLY INDUSTRY that needed Pasteur's help. In the mid-1800s, French silkmakers also faced a crisis. Silk is a kind of fine, soft cloth made from threads spun by silkworms. A mysterious disease was killing off the silkworms, and the lack of silk posed a major problem for the French clothing industry.

The chemist Jean-Baptiste Dumas came from the part of France where silk was produced. He asked Pasteur to head a group studying the silkworm problem. At the time, Pasteur knew nothing of silkworms or their diseases. When he pointed this out, Dumas replied, "So much the better! For ideas, you will have only those which shall come to you as a result of your own observations."[1] Pasteur accepted the challenge.

In June 1865, at age forty-two, Pasteur traveled from Paris to Alais. This town (now called Alès) in southern France lay in the heart of the silkworm region. Pasteur set up a research lab there. He returned to Alais every summer through 1869.

Pasteur quickly learned that one disease affecting the silkworms caused small black spots on their skin. Since these spots looked like grains of pepper, the disease was called *pébrine*—from *pébré*, a French slang word for pepper.

Just nine days after his arrival in Alais, however, Pasteur was called away. His father was very ill. By the time Pasteur reached Arbois, his father was already dead. The loss touched Pasteur deeply. He wrote: "Dear Marie, dear children, the dear grandfather is no more; we have taken him this morning to his last resting place, close to little Jeanne's."[2] Yet Pasteur also wrote that he must go back to Alais. His study of silkworms would be seriously set back if he did not return soon to his lab.

Once in Alais, Pasteur began studying both sick and healthy silkworms. When he looked at the sick worms under a microscope, he saw oval shapes. Pasteur didn't grasp the importance of these oval shapes at first. Finally he guessed that the silkworms were infected with some microbe. Proving this, however, took much hard work and many false starts.

Silkworms are actually the larva, or caterpillar, stage of a moth. This moth lays its eggs in early summer. Tiny silkworms hatch from the eggs. These worms eat almost constantly until they're fully grown. Then they spin silky cases called cocoons around themselves. Silk is made from the threads in these cocoons. While inside the cocoon, the worm changes into a pupa. After it emerges from the cocoon, the pupa changes into an adult moth, which mates and lays eggs. Then the whole life cycle begins again.

Pasteur showed that *pébrine* could be controlled by a process known as the egg-selection method. Some of the moths were checked under a microscope for signs of disease. If such signs were found, the moths and any eggs they had laid were destroyed. In this way, only healthy silkworms would be allowed to hatch.

Some people objected that a microscope was fine for scientists, but silkworm growers would never be able to use one. Pasteur responded: "There is in my laboratory a little girl eight years of age who has learned to use it without difficulty."[3] This little girl was his daughter Marie-Louise, who often helped out in the lab.

Edgar Bowers, an award-winning American poet, has written a poem titled "For Louis Pasteur." In it, Bowers describes Pasteur, who "for delight" was "Teaching his daughter to use a microscope/ And musing through a wonder."[4]

During 1866, Pasteur used the egg-selection method to pick batches of eggs that should have been healthy. As he expected, most of the silkworms that hatched from these eggs were free of disease. But some were not. These worms didn't have the skin spots seen in *pébrine*. Instead, they had soft, flabby bodies.

Pasteur finally showed that *pébrine* wasn't the only disease killing the silkworms. At least one other disease was attacking the worms as well. Often both diseases infected the same worm, which had just made things more confusing. Pasteur worked out a method for controlling the spread of this second disease as well.

In 1867, Pasteur came up with a bold way to show the usefulness of his methods. He sent a trade journal batches of silkworm eggs along with his predictions of which would be healthy. These predictions were sealed, to be opened only after the silkworms had hatched. Pasteur's predictions turned out to be correct.

These successes are all the more remarkable because they were made at a time of great sadness. Louis and Marie Pasteur's youngest child, Camille, died in September 1865, just months after the death of Pasteur's father. Camille was only two years old at the time. Then in May 1866, while working in Alais, Pasteur received word that his daughter Cécile was gravely ill with typhoid fever. She died days later, at age twelve.

In the years before vaccines and antibiotic drugs, such losses were all too common. Diseases such as typhoid fever, diphtheria, pertussis (also called whooping cough), and scarlet fever were frequent killers of children. Yet the death of a child was every bit as painful then as it is today. Pasteur was deeply affected by the deaths of his children. In a letter to his wife, he mourned, "Our beloved children die one after another!"[5]

Still, Pasteur continued to work long hours at Alais. In addition to his lab there, he set up a silkworm farm for testing his ideas. There was always much to do. There were worms to be raised and eggs to be collected. There were countless experiments to be run. The mulberry leaves that the silkworms ate had to be harvested, and the mice that liked to eat the silkworms had to be controlled. In the evenings, Pasteur would dictate letters, journal articles, and book chapters to his busy wife.

Each fall, Pasteur returned to Paris, where he

Louis Pasteur dictating a paper to Marie at Alais. While at Alais, Pasteur would remedy an epidemic that was causing the death of silkworms, and thus hurting the French economy.

continued to teach students and do research at the École Normale. His duties there also included helping run the school itself. He oversaw such matters as the students' rooms and food, and he enforced the school's rules. Pasteur was very strict. This made him unpopular with many students.[6]

In 1867, Pasteur lost his old job at the École Normale after a student protest. The people in charge didn't want to lose such a respected scientist, so they gave Pasteur a new job at the École Normale: director of an enlarged chemistry lab. He was also made professor of chemistry at the Sorbonne University.

The long hours and heavy duties must have taken a toll. In October 1868, when he was forty-five, Pasteur suffered a stroke. A stroke occurs when a blood vessel to the brain breaks or becomes blocked. The sudden loss of brain function can lead to a number of effects, including paralysis, the loss of voluntary movement in part of the body.

Just after the stroke, Pasteur was completely

unable to move the left side of his body. Slowly, much of his strength returned. But he never totally regained his prior ability to speak, walk, and work with his hands. From that time on, Pasteur needed the help of assistants to carry out some of his experiments. As you might expect, Pasteur had a reputation for being as demanding of his assistants as he was of himself.

Not even a stroke could stop Pasteur's work for long. In 1869, he was invited to Villa Vicentina, an estate in Austria owned by a prince. Silkworms were grown there. Pasteur was asked to tackle the estate's *pébrine* problem.

Life at Villa Vicentina was more restful for Pasteur. He took walks and carriage rides. He even sometimes walked the ponies that were the delight of his two surviving children, Jean-Baptiste and Marie-Louise. In this peaceful setting, Pasteur finished writing a book on silkworm diseases. And the next summer, thanks to Pasteur's efforts, Villa Vicentina had one of its best silkworm crops ever.

9

The Tiniest Enemies

MOST PEOPLE WOULDN'T THINK THAT silkworms and humans have much in common. Pasteur came to believe otherwise. If microbes could cause diseases in worms, he reasoned, surely they could cause human diseases as well.

In the seventeenth century, the Dutch scientist Antoni van Leeuwenhoek had described "tiny animals" that he viewed with simple microscopes. Such microorganisms were still a mystery, though. People didn't know that some could cause disease. In fact, one popular theory stated that disease was caused by poisonous fumes that were given off by decaying matter and blown about by the wind.

Pasteur's work with silkworms led him to the brink of some of his most important discoveries. Then history interfered. In 1870, France became involved in a war with Prussia, a German state. The war forced Pasteur to leave Paris, and his work there, behind. He took his family to Arbois until the war's end.

Louis and Marie Pasteur's son, Jean-Baptiste, was now a young man. He joined the French army. Pasteur waited anxiously for news of his son. Finally, he could stand the worry no longer. He traveled to a town near the Swiss border, where Jean-Baptiste's unit was thought to be. The French soldiers Pasteur found there were a sorry sight indeed. They were suffering from diseases, injuries, and frozen feet.

Happily, Pasteur found his own son alive, if not quite well. With his parents' care, Jean-Baptiste soon recovered from his illness. But Pasteur never forgot the grim scene of hundreds of sick and injured soldiers.

Pasteur always loved his country dearly. He was so upset by the Prussian siege of Paris that he returned an honorary doctor's degree given to him by a German university. France's defeat in 1871 came as a blow to Pasteur.

After the war, Pasteur was offered a job as a chemistry professor at an Italian university. It would have meant more money for Pasteur, but he turned down the job. He refused to leave France in his country's time of need.

Instead, Pasteur chose to help France in an unusual way. German beer was widely regarded as some of the best in the world. Pasteur decided to study beer, with the aim of making French beer as good as the German kind.

This idea came to Pasteur while he was visiting Émile Duclaux, a former student. Duclaux was now a professor in a French town with a nearby brewery, a place where beer is made. Pasteur saw this as a chance to expand his earlier work on fermentation. Soon he had shown that changes in beer, like those in wine, were due to microorganisms. These changes could also be prevented by pasteurization.

Even after he returned to the École Normale in Paris, Pasteur kept studying beer and fermentation. He continued this research until 1877.

Pasteur's patriotism showed up in another way around this time. In 1876, he decided to run for the Senate. He thought that if he were elected, he could help France regain its place as a center of learning. In his words: "If you honor me with your vote, I shall represent science in all its purity, dignity, and independence in the Senate."[1] Pasteur proved to be a poor candidate, though. He was badly defeated in the election.

In 1877, Pasteur's interests took a new turn. He began focusing on the causes of disease. Twenty years before, Pasteur had first laid out his germ theory of fermentation. This set the stage for the even more important germ theory of disease. The theory stated that many diseases are caused by microbes. As with fermentation, each such disease can be linked to a particular kind of microbe.

Pasteur wasn't the only scientist of his day working on these germ theories. His main rival was Robert Koch, a German doctor. Koch worked out a method for showing which type of bacteria causes a certain disease. Using this method, he was able to show in 1876 that a particular kind of bacteria causes anthrax, a deadly disease that infects cattle and sheep and can be spread to humans.

A great burst of progress followed. Between 1877 and 1888, Pasteur himself discovered the microbes that cause half a dozen animal and human diseases. In one case, he set about finding the source of a painful skin disease that bothered Émile Duclaux, his former student. Duclaux suffered from furunculosis, a skin disease that leads to painful, pus-filled swellings called boils. Pasteur traced Duclaux's problem to a particular type of *Staphylococcus* bacteria.

Pasteur was not willing to stop there. As always, he wanted to put his findings to use solving practical problems. He suggested that

Robert Koch (above) and Pasteur are both credited with proving the germ theory of disease.

certain diseases could be prevented by getting rid of the microbes that cause them.

One person who read about Pasteur's ideas was Joseph Lister, an English doctor. He grew convinced that microbes were causing the deaths of many patients who had surgery—operations to treat disease. Lister began covering surgical wounds with bandages that had been treated with a chemical compound called carbolic acid. This was done to kill any microbes around the wound. Lister also sprayed carbolic acid around the entire area where the surgery was done. As a result, fewer wounds became infected, and more surgical patients survived.

Lister is often considered the father of modern surgery. He was always quick to admit his debt to Pasteur's writings. In an 1874 letter, Lister noted that his own ideas were based on Pasteur's germ theory. He invited Pasteur to visit his hospital, to see "how largely mankind is being benefited by your labours."[2]

Today doctors try to keep microbes away from surgical wounds in the first place instead of just trying to kill them. They wash their hands thoroughly before an operation, and they wear germ-free gloves and gowns. They also wear masks to help prevent the spread of microbes through the air. In addition, operating rooms are kept as clean as possible. Such measures have saved countless lives.

It's not surprising that Pasteur worried about microbes in his own life. Sometimes he took this concern a bit too far. He often refused to shake hands for fear of catching an illness. And at the dinner table, he always wiped his glass and silverware in the hopes of getting rid of any dirt that might be there.

You might not go to such lengths. Yet you do know you should cover your mouth when you cough to keep from spreading microbes through the air, and you know you should wash your hands before cooking to keep from passing microbes on your skin. People didn't always know how important microbes are, though. It was hard for them to believe something so tiny could be so powerful. Pasteur helped to change all that.

Warfare Against Germs

PASTEUR WASN'T SATISFIED JUST TO learn more about microbes. He wanted to fight back against them, too.[1] He dreamed that someday there would be a way to prevent infectious diseases. These are diseases that are caused by microbes and can be spread from one living thing to another. Many infectious diseases can be spread from human to human, or animal to human, or animal to animal.

In 1879, a disease called chicken cholera raged through the barnyards of France. Wherever it struck, it killed most of the chickens within a few days. Pasteur began to study the microbe that causes chicken cholera by culturing it, growing it in the lab in a special substance. He soon found that, when healthy chickens were given a shot of the chicken cholera culture, they would die within a day or two.

That summer, Pasteur took a vacation, heading for Arbois. He left his cultures in the care of his lab assistants. One of those assistants was Émile Roux, who later became one of Pasteur's most important coworkers.

Legend has it that the lab assistants took a vacation, too. They left the cultures unattended for several weeks. It's also possible that Roux left the cultures alone on purpose to see what would happen to them. In any case, Pasteur returned from Arbois to find a lab full of old, dried-out cultures.

When chickens were injected with some of this old chicken cholera culture, they stayed healthy. It seemed the culture had lost its ability to cause disease. Then something even more surprising happened. Both these chickens and some new ones were injected with fresh culture.

The new chickens soon died, but to everyone's amazement, most that had previously received the old culture remained well.

The assistants were worried. What would Pasteur's reaction be? Pasteur was silent for a few minutes, as he thought about what had occurred. Then he exclaimed, "Don't you see that these animals have been vaccinated!"[2] A vaccinated animal or person is given a vaccine, a preparation of weakened or killed microbes that prevents a disease.

At the time, only one type of vaccination was used. People in England had noticed that dairymaids who got cowpox, a skin disease spread to humans by infected cows, later were less likely to get smallpox, a similar but more serious disease that also caused skin sores.

An English doctor named Edward Jenner set out to study this matter. In 1796, Jenner gave the first medical vaccination. He took the pus from a cowpox sore and put it into the arm of a healthy boy. As expected, the boy soon came down with cowpox. Later, Jenner gave the boy a dose of smallpox pus. It had no effect. Having had cowpox, the boy was protected against the deadlier disease.

Pasteur guessed that something along the same line had happened to his chickens. The old culture, while unable to cause chicken cholera, was still somehow able to protect the chickens from catching the disease later. Pasteur experimented some more. He thought that leaving chicken cholera culture to sit in the air for a prolonged time was the key. This weakened the culture enough to make it safe.

Pasteur announced the discovery of a chicken cholera vaccine in 1880. He hoped his method might work to create vaccines for other diseases, too. In particular, he hoped it would work for anthrax. Pasteur had been studying anthrax since 1877, building on the findings of the German doctor Robert Koch.

At the time, anthrax was a major killer of sheep. French farmers lost many millions of francs each year because of it. Shepherds had noticed that sheep that grazed in certain fields

Pasteur with two rabbits. The scientist used animals for many of his experiments on microbes and vaccines.

were more likely to get the disease. This was true even when the fields had been abandoned for years. Were the fields cursed?

Pasteur thought not. He knew that the shepherds usually buried dead animals in the fields where they had died. He also knew what Koch had found: The anthrax microbe has a resting form that can survive for long periods without losing its ability to cause disease. Finally, Pasteur had seen signs of earthworms over the pits where animals were buried. He put these pieces together to solve the puzzle. Pasteur showed that earthworms were bringing the anthrax bacteria up from the pits to the surface of the soil. Animals who grazed there could then catch the disease.

The fields weren't cursed. They just held bacteria. Armed with these facts, Pasteur offered his advice. He told shepherds either to burn dead animals or to bury them in spots where sheep and cattle would never graze.

By 1881, Pasteur had produced an anthrax vaccine. It was time to put this new vaccine to the test. Pasteur had always had a flair for the dramatic when it came to his work. Now he agreed to a public demonstration.

The historic test took place on a farm at Pouilly-le-Fort, a village southeast of Paris. On May 5, 24 sheep, six cows, and one goat were given Pasteur's vaccine against anthrax.[3] They were vaccinated again twelve days later. Then on May 31, all of the vaccinated animals were injected with anthrax culture. So were twenty-four unvaccinated sheep, four unvaccinated cows, and one unvaccinated goat.[4]

This was the world's first public test of a vaccine made in a lab. Pasteur was not modest in his claims. He predicted that the vaccinated animals would all survive, while the unvaccinated animals would all sicken and die. Now there was nothing left to do but wait and see if his bold predictions would come true.

There were some tense moments the next day. What if Pasteur was wrong? It would be a disaster for his career. His fear, he told his wife and helpers, was that "this will be the ruin of all my work and of all my hopes!"[5]

On June 2, Pasteur returned to the farm to find out the results of his experiment. A crowd of more than two hundred officials, veterinarians, farmers, and others had already gathered there. Among them was a reporter from a London newspaper. Thanks to his widely read reports, the eyes of the world were on Pasteur that day.

When Pasteur arrived, the crowd burst into applause. His test had been a great success. All of the vaccinated animals were well, but twenty-one of the unvaccinated sheep and the lone unvaccinated goat were dead. The other three unvaccinated sheep died by day's end, and the four unvaccinated cows all had a fever and swelling.

Pasteur's triumph was complete. Soon after the test, his lab began to make and sell anthrax vaccine to farmers and veterinarians. By the end of the century, millions of sheep and thousands of cows had been vaccinated.

Ever since Pasteur had suffered his stroke, his

doctor had urged him to slow down. Pasteur would hear nothing of it. Now at least he had someone new to help him. In 1879, Louis and Marie Pasteur's daughter Marie-Louise had married René Vallery-Radot. He was a devoted son-in-law, often going with Pasteur to scientific meetings. Five years after Pasteur's death, Vallery-Radot published a book about Pasteur's life.

In 1881, at age fifty-eight, Pasteur had reached one of the high points of his career, but he wanted more. He had shown that his vaccines would work in livestock. Now he wanted to prove that they could help people, too.

Victory Over Rabies

IN PASTEUR'S DAY, INFECTIOUS DISEASES took a terrible toll on human life. Little was known about how to prevent them. Pasteur wanted to change that. Even before his test of the anthrax vaccine, he had already chosen his next target. Pasteur aimed to make a vaccine against the deadly disease called rabies.

Rabies in humans has always been rare. In the 1870s, it probably killed fewer than fifty people a year in France. Still, it has always inspired terror. People catch rabies from the bite of an infected animal, often a dog. The image of the "mad dog," attacking anyone in its path, strikes fear in the hearts of many.

In addition, death by rabies is a particularly unpleasant way to die. In humans, rabies often leads to headaches and extreme restlessness. This is typically followed by loss of the ability to use the muscles, and finally death.

Many diseases can only be prevented if the vaccine is given before a person comes into

Rabies is also known as hydrophobia, meaning "fear of water." A "mad dog" is causing panic in the streets of London in this 1826 cartoon.

contact with the disease. Rabies is different. It develops slowly, usually taking a month or two from the time a person is bitten until the effects start. This means that there is enough time to give the vaccine after a person has already been bitten.

Pasteur began seriously studying rabies in 1880. He took the spinal cords of rabbits that had died of the disease. The spinal cord is a cord of nerve tissue that runs through the backbone. Since rabies affects nerve tissue, the cords carried the microbe that causes the disease. Pasteur stored these cords for two weeks in flasks full of clean, dry air. This made them almost harmless. A famous painting by Paul Edelfelt (see page 40) shows Pasteur looking at one of these flasks in his lab at the École Normale.

Pasteur had already developed a method of giving vaccines in a series of shots. If the microbes in a vaccine aren't weakened enough, they can actually cause a disease, rather than prevent it. However, if the microbes aren't strong enough, the vaccine may not work. In his studies

Pasteur checks rabbits that have been injected with the rabies microbe in this 1888 illustration.

of chicken cholera and anthrax, Pasteur had learned to give a series of shots, starting with the weakest one and building up to the strongest. This let the animals gradually build up defenses against the disease.

In his studies of rabies, Pasteur gave a series of shots of dried spinal cord to healthy dogs. The first shot contained cord that had been dried for the full fourteen days. It was too weak to make the dogs sick. The next shot contained cord that had been dried for a slightly shorter time and so was a little stronger. Each shot that followed was stronger still. Finally, the dogs were given shots of cord so fresh it should have caused the disease. But the dogs stayed well. Pasteur's method of vaccination had worked.

Pasteur was helped in this research by Émile Roux. The men needed a place to house the many animals used in their experiments. The city of Paris first let Pasteur have some land near his lab for this purpose. A few years later, Pasteur began to use the old stables at Villeneuve l'Étang, a park west of Paris. The stables were turned into a large dog kennel. A lab and living space were soon added, too.

By this time, Pasteur had successfully vaccinated fifty dogs without a single failure. The next step was to try the vaccine in humans.

On July 6, 1885, three worried visitors came to see Pasteur. One was a nine-year-old boy named Joseph Meister. Two days before, Joseph had been attacked by a dog with rabies. He was bitten at least a dozen times. He had deep wounds on his hands and legs, some so bad that he could barely walk. Joseph's mother and the dog's owner had brought the boy by train to Paris to seek Pasteur's help.

Pasteur faced one of the toughest decisions of his life. Without the vaccine, Joseph would almost certainly die. Pasteur thought he could probably save the boy. But he couldn't be sure. After all, this vaccine hadn't been tested on a human. There was always a small risk that it would actually make matters worse.

Pasteur asked for advice from two doctors. After seeing the boy, they agreed that Joseph had little chance of survival without the treatment. That's when Pasteur made up his mind. He had to try his best to save Joseph's life.

Later that same night, Joseph received his first shot of vaccine. Over the next eleven days, he was given twelve more shots, each slightly stronger than the one before. The last shot contained cord that had been taken just the day before from a rabbit that died of rabies. Afterward, Pasteur watched the boy anxiously for

Joseph Meister in 1885. Meister was the first to receive the rabies vaccine.

signs of the disease. Pasteur was so worried that he had trouble sleeping at night. When Joseph returned home, Pasteur sent him stamped envelopes so that Joseph could write often.

As the months passed, however, Pasteur's fears began to fade. The vaccine had worked! Joseph had escaped a horrible death.

In October, a second boy came to see Pasteur. He was Jean-Baptiste Jupille, a fifteen-year-old shepherd. Jean-Baptiste lived in a village near Arbois. The village mayor had written to Pasteur, telling him of the boy's bravery.

Jean-Baptiste and several younger shepherds had been watching over their sheep in a meadow when a dog with rabies attacked. Jean-Baptiste had rushed to protect the younger boys. He fought and killed the dog, but during the struggle, he was badly bitten. Without Pasteur's help, Jean-Baptiste seemed doomed.

Pasteur wrote back right away, offering to treat Jean-Baptiste. The mayor put the boy on the next train to Paris. On October 20, Jean-Baptiste received his first shot of vaccine. But it

Jean-Baptiste Jupille in 1885. Jupille contracted rabies after being bitten by a dog while protecting younger children.

was six days since the attack had occurred. Would the treatment be too late? Once again, Pasteur spent many hours worrying. As before, though, the vaccine did its job. Jean-Baptiste stayed free of rabies.

The world was thrilled by these dramatic success stories. At age sixty-two, Pasteur had achieved his greatest fame yet. By October 1886, just fifteen months after Joseph's treatment, nearly twenty-five hundred people had received the rabies vaccine.

Among them were four boys from Newark, New Jersey, who had been bitten by a dog with rabies in December 1885. They were put on a ship for Paris, where they received the new vaccine. American newspapers carried excited reports on their progress. All of them escaped the disease. When they arrived back in the United States, they were hailed as heroes. The boys were so famous for a time that people even paid to see them at state fairs and carnivals.

Not everyone was so impressed, however. At every stage of his career, Pasteur had faced some critics. This time was no different. Some people claimed that his rabies vaccine was useless or even dangerous.

Pasteur was forced to defend his treatment against these serious charges. His health suffered under the strain. He began to show signs of heart trouble. In November 1886, his doctors sent him away from Paris for a period of rest.

At last, the English Commission on Rabies decided to study the issue. In 1887, the commission presented its report. It found that Pasteur's new treatment had indeed saved many lives. This report did much to silence the critics.

Today people protect themselves and their pets against rabies by getting their dogs and cats vaccinated. However, it's still possible to catch the disease from wild animals and unvaccinated pets. If a person is bitten by an animal that may be infected, a series of shots must still be given. But there have been some improvements since Pasteur's day. Fewer shots may be needed, and they are less painful.[1]

Vaccines have now been developed to fight a

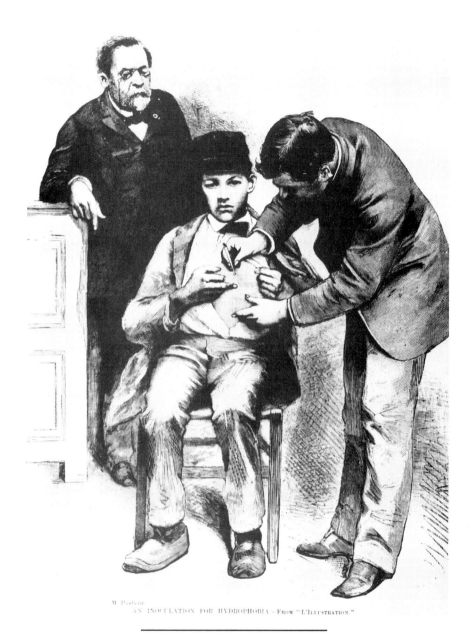

M. Pasteur.
AN INOCULATION FOR HYDROPHOBIA – From "L'Illustration."

Jean-Baptiste Jupille getting a shot of the rabies vaccine. Pasteur is watching in this drawing from a French magazine.

number of infectious diseases. Among them is typhoid fever, the illness that killed two of Louis and Marie Pasteur's daughters. Children in the United States receive several kinds of vaccinations beginning soon after birth. As a result, some once-common diseases have become uncommon in the United States and many other countries. These include killers of children such as diphtheria and pertussis.

The greatest success of all has been achieved with smallpox. By the late 1970s, the disease itself had been completely wiped off the earth. The only place the smallpox microbe now exists is in two labs, one at the Centers for Disease Control and Prevention in Atlanta, Georgia, and the other in Koltsovo, Russia.[2]

A Center for Science

PEOPLE WERE GRATEFUL TO PASTEUR for developing the rabies vaccine. Patients from around the world flocked to his lab to get the new treatment. Money to fund his work also began to pour into Paris. Soon more than 2 million francs had been collected. This money was used to set up the Pasteur Institute. It was to be a center for the treatment and study of rabies and other problems in microbiology.

By 1888, the new institute was ready. A ceremony marking its opening was held on November 14. It was a grand occasion. Even the French president came. Pasteur had planned to give a short speech, but at the last minute, he was overcome by emotion. He asked his son, Jean-Baptiste, to read it instead.

In this speech, Pasteur thanked the people of the country he loved so dearly. Jean-Baptiste read: "Never has a Frenchman addressing himself to other Frenchmen been more profoundly moved than I am at this moment."[1]

Pasteur served as director of the Pasteur Institute until his death in 1895. Sadly, though, he was not able to do much research of his own at the institute that bore his name. In October 1887, he had suffered two small strokes. From that point on, his health and strength seemed to drain slowly away.

Yet Pasteur still took great interest in the work being done at the institute. He and his wife moved into an apartment there, located next to the labs. Today the apartment where they lived has been turned into a museum. Visitors can see the bedroom, dining room, and study, along with Pasteur's desk and books.[2]

It was up to others to carry on the work

Pasteur at about age sixty-seven.

Pasteur had begun. The next Pasteur Institute directors who followed Pasteur were Émile Duclaux and Émile Roux. These men had been two of Pasteur's closest coworkers.

Over the years, eight Pasteur Institute scientists have been awarded Nobel Prizes in science. These are among the world's most prestigious awards. In 1891, the first of many overseas branches of the institute was opened in Saigon, a city in southern Vietnam now known as Ho Chi Minh City. In 1900, Roux helped set up a Pasteur Institute hospital in Paris that is still in use.

Today the Pasteur Institute is involved in research on such topics as infectious diseases, vaccines, AIDS, cancer, and allergies. The main center is still located in Paris. In addition to being a research facility, it is a teaching center. It also houses the largest microbiology library in France. Outside of Paris, there is now a worldwide network of twenty-seven institutes, nineteen of which bear the name Pasteur.[3]

A well-known statue now stands outside the

The New York branch of the Pasteur Institute. The opening of this building was celebrated in October 1893.

Paris Institute. It depicts Jean-Baptiste Jupille, the young shepherd who was saved by Pasteur's rabies vaccine. The statue shows Jean-Baptiste in his heroic struggle against a dog with rabies.

Pasteur received many honors late in life. Perhaps the most notable was a celebration on December 27, 1892, held at the Sorbonne University on the day of Pasteur's seventieth birthday. Pasteur, who was quite weak by this time, was led into the theater on the arm of the French president. The audience was filled with

Pasteur's seventieth birthday at the Sorbonne University. Pasteur, leaning on the arm of the French President, is greeted by Joseph Lister.

former students and assistants, officials, scientists, and other admirers.

Several speakers honored Pasteur's life and work. One was Joseph Lister, who told how Pasteur's writings had helped him revolutionize surgery. Pasteur himself was too ill to speak. Once again, his son read for him. He urged the young people in the crowd: "Live in the serene peace of laboratories and libraries."[4]

The Legacy of Pasteur

PASTEUR WAS A KIND MAN, BUT HE could be stern. He liked to work silently in his lab. He told his assistants what to do, but he rarely shared his deeper thoughts with them. He liked for them to work in silence, too. He also discouraged outsiders from visiting the lab. Pasteur hated to be disturbed while he was busy.

As his body grew weaker with age, however, his manner became gentler. People who knew Pasteur as an old man have said he appeared sad. His grandson, Pasteur Vallery-Radot, later described him this way: "I see again that face, that appeared to be carved from a block of granite—that high and large forehead, those grayish-green eyes, with such a deep and kind look. . . . He seemed to me serious and sad."[1]

As death grew nearer, Pasteur became ever more tender toward his family. His daughter Marie-Louise and her husband lived nearby with their two children. Pasteur visited every afternoon. He took great joy in his grandchildren. In a note to his granddaughter, Camille Vallery-Radot, he wrote: "During these ten years, I believe, I never thought of you without loving you more and more."[2]

Pasteur's health continued to fail. In June 1895, he moved to Villeneuve l'Étang, where the dog kennel was located. There he would try to rest and recover, surrounded by his loved ones and the big trees of the park.

But he only grew worse. Speech became more and more difficult for him. His weakness and inability to move gradually increased. When he was offered a glass of milk on September 27, he said his last words: "I cannot."[3] Pasteur died late

Pasteur with his granddaughter, Camille Vallery-Radot. Toward the end of his life, Pasteur received much enjoyment from spending time with his grandchildren.

the next afternoon, on September 28, 1895. He was seventy-two years old.

A grand funeral was held for Pasteur on October 5. It was paid for by the French government. A church service was conducted at the famous Cathedral of Notre-Dame in Paris. A distinguished crowd attended. Among those who came were the French president, a Russian grand duke, and a Greek prince.

After the church service, the crowd moved through the streets of Paris to the Pasteur Institute. Solemn throngs of ordinary people lined the way. They, too, wanted to pay their last respects to this national hero.

Pasteur's body was buried at the Pasteur Institute. His tomb lies in an elaborate chapel there. It is decorated in marble, gold, and colorful mosaics that picture some of his discoveries. At the entrance are these words: "Blessed is the Man who Carries in his Soul a God, a Beautiful Ideal that he Obeys—Ideal of Art, Ideal of Science, Ideal of the Fatherland, Ideal of the Virtues of the Gospel."[4]

At the start of World War II, the gatekeeper at the Pasteur Institute was none other than Joseph Meister. Fifty-five years earlier, Meister had been saved by Pastuer's rabies vaccine. After German soldiers took over Paris in 1940, Meister killed himself. Some people claim he did this to keep from having to open Pasteur's tomb for the German soldiers.[5] Other people, including Meister's own daughter, doubt this is the real reason. They think Meister was upset about the war. In fact, German soldiers did ask to see Pasteur's tomb, but they did no harm. They just wanted to see where the scientist was buried.[6]

Since Pasteur's death, his life story has been retold many times. In 1900, his son-in-law, René Vallery-Radot, published a lengthy biography. Its title, in English, is *The Life of Pasteur*. It is still the most detailed look at Pasteur's life. In 1950, the microbiologist René Dubos published another important biography, *Louis Pasteur: Free Lance of Science*. A number of other books have also appeared.

Even Hollywood was drawn to the drama of

Pasteur's life. The result was an excellent 1936 American movie called *The Story of Louis Pasteur*. The actor Paul Muni won an Oscar for his performance in that film.[7]

It has now been more than a century since Pasteur's death, but his name lives on in some unexpected places. Throughout France, there are streets, schools, hospitals, and labs that bear the name Pasteur. In Paris, a major street is called Boulevard Pasteur, and a main subway station is called Station Pasteur. The scientist's name has also been given to a village in Algeria and a district in Canada.

In addition, several scientific terms are based on Pasteur's name. Pasteurization is the most familiar. The Pasteur effect is a blocking of fermentation that occurs when much oxygen is present. A particular group of bacteria are known by the name Pasteurella, and the disease they cause is called pasteurellosis.

Pasteur's image can be seen in a variety of places as well. A statue of the great man stands in the courtyard of the Sorbonne University. In the past, Pasteur's face also graced the five-franc bill and a postage stamp in France.

The list of Pasteur's achievements is a long and impressive one. He gave us pasteurization and the rabies vaccine. He helped us understand

A bust of Pasteur surrounded by symbols of his career. Among the items shown are a microscope, a bottle of wine, a picture of swan-necked flasks, photographs of Joseph Meister and Jean-Baptiste Jupille, and various papers and books.

how microbes cause disease. He also helped found the fields of stereochemistry and microbiology. In addition, Pasteur was a pioneer in the vaccination of humans and animals. The scientists who followed his lead made discoveries that have saved the lives of millions of people and spared many millions more from illness and suffering.

Yet Pasteur was not only a great scientist. He was also a great man who devoted himself to the welfare of humankind. This, above all else, is the reason he is still revered.

In Pasteur's Footsteps

PASTEUR WAS ALWAYS ALERT. THIS HELPED him see things that other people missed, such as the facets on crystals. It also helped him notice things that other people had seen but ignored, such as the behavior of bacteria under a microscope. By keeping your own eyes and mind open, you can follow in Pasteur's footsteps.

Do these activities. Then try to answer the questions that follow them.

Crystal Clear

Would you like to examine the shapes of crystals for yourself? You can grow your own crystals easily by following these steps.

Materials needed:

- 6 pieces of charcoal (the kind used for cooking outdoors)

- 6 tablespoons of water

- 6 tablespoons of laundry bluing

- 1 tablespoon of ammonia

- 6 teaspoons of salt

- a shallow pan

CAUTION: Laundry bluing and ammonia can be dangerous if they get in your eyes or on your skin. Have an adult help you with this experiment.

Procedure:

Put the charcoal pieces in the pan. Mix the water, bluing, ammonia, and salt. Then pour this mixture over the charcoal pieces. Place the pan in a warm spot so that the water dries up quickly.

Once the water has dried up, you should see crystals left behind. To get a better look at them, you can use a magnifying glass.

Questions:

What crystal shapes do you see? Can you draw the shapes, the way Pasteur did? How accurate are your drawings?

Yeast Feast

Yeast grows quickly in the presence of sugar. It causes the sugar to change into alcohol and the gas carbon dioxide.

Materials needed:

- 1 package of powdered yeast
- 1 tablespoon of sugar
- 2 cups of warm water
- a glass soda bottle
- a balloon

Procedure:

Mix the yeast and sugar in one cup of warm water. Make sure that the water is warm, not hot. Pour this solution into the bottle. Then add the other cup of warm water. After squeezing any air out of the balloon, stretch its neck over the mouth of the bottle. Then set the bottle in a warm, dark spot for three to four days, and watch what happens. Fermentation should soon cause some noticeable effects.

Check the bottle daily. You should see changes that are due to carbon dioxide, the same gas that causes bread to rise.

Questions:

Do you see bubbles being formed in the liquid? Is the balloon partly inflated? How do your answers change from day to day?

Dirty Tricks

You know that it's important to wash your hands before eating or cooking to keep from spreading microbes. This activity shows why.

Materials needed:

- 2 small potatoes
- a potato peeler
- 2 jars with lids that seal

The potatoes should be washed and the peeler and jars should be boiled to get rid of as many microbes on their surfaces as possible.

CAUTION: Boiling water is dangerous. Have an adult boil the peeler and jars.

Procedure:

Leave your hands unwashed for several hours. Then peel one of the potatoes and put it in a jar. Wash the peeler. Next, scrub your hands well.

Then peel the other potato and put it in the other jar. Seal both jars. Label the first one "unwashed hands" and the second one "washed hands." Then leave both jars in a warm spot where they can be watched for several days.

Check the jars daily without removing their lids. After a few days, you'll probably notice the growth of furry-looking mold on one or both potatoes. Mold grows from spores, special kinds of cells that are too small to be seen with the naked eye.

Questions:

Do you see furry-looking mold growing on the potato in the "unwashed hands" jar? In the "washed hands" jar? Which potato has more mold on it?

Your unwashed hands should have carried more mold spores than your washed hands. You couldn't see the spores on your dirty hands, any more than you can see the bacteria and other microbes there. But such microorganisms can still do harm. That's why it's important to wash your hands before handling food.

Chronology

1822—December 27: Louis Pasteur is born to Jean-Joseph and Jeanne Pasteur in Dôle, France.

1827—Pasteur family moves to Arbois.

1839–42—Pasteur attends the Royal College of Besançon.

1842–43—Attends the Lycée Saint-Louis in Paris.

1843–48—Studies chemistry at the École Normale in Paris.

1847—Completes his Doctor of Science degree.

1848—April: Discovers the role of facets on crystals.

May: Jeanne Pasteur, Louis Pasteur's mother, dies.

1849–54—Pasteur teaches chemistry at the University of Strasbourg.

1849—May 29: Pasteur marries Marie Laurent in Strasbourg.

1850—Daughter Jeanne Pasteur is born.

1851—Son Jean-Baptiste Pasteur is born.

1853—Daughter Cécile Pasteur is born.

1854–57—Pasteur is dean of sciences at the University of Lille.

1857—Introduces his germ theory of fermentation.

1857–67—Serves as director of scientific studies at the École Normale.

1858—Daughter Marie-Louise Pasteur is born.

1859—Daughter Jeanne Pasteur dies.

1861—Pasteur discovers anaerobic bacteria.

1863–67—Teaches science at the École des Beaux-Arts in Paris.

1863—Daughter Camille Pasteur is born.

1864—Pasteur gives famous lecture on spontaneous generation.

1865–69—Studies silkworm diseases in Alais.

1865—Conducts studies on pasteurization.

June: Jean-Joseph Pasteur, Louis Pasteur's father, dies.

September: Daughter Camille Pasteur dies.

1866—Daughter Cécile Pasteur dies.

1867–88—Pasteur is director of a chemistry lab at the École Normale.

1867–74—Teaches chemistry at the Sorbonne University in Paris.

1868—Suffers his first stroke.

1870–71—France is defeated in a war with Prussia.

1880—Pasteur announces the discovery of a chicken cholera vaccine.

1881—Conducts a public test of his anthrax vaccine at Pouilly-le-Fort.

1885—July: Joseph Meister receives the rabies vaccine.

October: Jean-Baptiste Jupille receives the rabies vaccine.

1887—July: The English Commission on Rabies issues its report on the vaccine.

October: Pasteur suffers two small strokes.

1888—November 14: The Pasteur Institute holds its opening ceremony.

1888–95—Pasteur is director of the Pasteur Institute in Paris.

1892—Is honored on his birthday at the Sorbonne University.

1895—September 28: Louis Pasteur dies at Villeneuve l'Étang at age seventy-two.

October 5: Pasteur's funeral is held.

Chapter Notes

Chapter 1

1. Gerald L. Geison, *The Private Science of Louis Pasteur* (Princeton, N.J.: Princeton University Press, 1995), p. 22.

2. Ibid., p. 23.

3. Ibid., pp. 265–266.

4. Ibid., pp. 16–17.

5. Ibid., p. 40.

Chapter 2

1. For more information on the museum, write: La Maison de Louis Pasteur, 83 rue de Courcelles, 39600 Arbois, France.

2. René Dubos, *Pasteur and Modern Science,* ed. Thomas D. Brock (Madison, Wis.: Science Tech, 1988), p. 7.

3. René Dubos, *Louis Pasteur: Free Lance of Science* (New York: Da Capo, 1960), p. xix.

4. Gerald L. Geison, *The Private Science of Louis Pasteur* (Princeton, N.J.: Princeton University Press, 1995), pp. 177–178.

5. René Vallery-Radot, *The Life of Pasteur,* trans. Mrs. R. L. Devonshire (Garden City, N.Y.: Doubleday, Page, 1927), pp. 11–12.

Chapter 3

1. Pasteur Vallery-Radot, *Louis Pasteur: A Great Life in Brief,* trans. Alfred Joseph (New York: Alfred A. Knopf, 1970), p. 16.

2. René Vallery-Radot, *The Life of Pasteur,* trans. Mrs. R. L. Devonshire (Garden City, N.Y.: Doubleday, Page, 1927), p. 14.

3. Pasteur Vallery-Radot, p. 25.

4. René Vallery-Radot, pp. 21–22.

5. Ibid., p. 32.

Chapter 4

1. René Vallery-Radot, *The Life of Pasteur,* trans. Mrs. R. L. Devonshire (Garden City, N.Y.: Doubleday, Page, 1927), p. 39.

2. René Dubos, *Pasteur and Modern Science,* ed. Thomas D. Brock (Madison, Wis.: Science Tech, 1988), p. 19.

3. Ibid., p. 20.

4. Gerald L. Geison, *The Private Science of Louis Pasteur* (Princeton, N.J.: Princeton University Press, 1995), p. 25

5. Pasteur Vallery-Radot, *Louis Pasteur: A Great Life in Brief,* trans. Alfred Joseph (New York: Alfred A. Knopf, 1970), p. 37.

6. Ibid., p. 39.

7. Geison, p. 46.

8. Ibid., p. 139.

Chapter 5

1. Pasteur Vallery-Radot, *Louis Pasteur: A Great Life in Brief,* trans. Alfred Joseph (New York: Alfred A. Knopf, 1970), p. 54.

Chapter 6

1. Pasteur Vallery-Radot, *Louis Pasteur: A Great Life in Brief,* trans. Alfred Joseph (New York: Alfred A. Knopf, 1970), p. 60.

2. René Dubos, *Louis Pasteur: Free Lance of Science* (New York: Da Capo, 1960), p. 177.

Chapter 7

1. For more information on pasteurized milk, write: National Dairy Board, 10255 West Higgins Road, Suite 900, Rosemont, IL 60018-5616.

Chapter 8

1. René Dubos, *Pasteur and Modern Science,* ed. Thomas D. Brock (Madison, Wis.: Science Tech, 1988), p. 91.

2. René Vallery-Radot, *The Life of Pasteur,* trans. Mrs. R. L. Devonshire (Garden City, N.Y.: Doubleday, Page, 1927), p. 118.

3. René Dubos, *Louis Pasteur: Free Lance of Science* (New York: Da Capo, 1960), p. 218.

4. Edgar Bowers, *For Louis Pasteur* (Princeton, N.J.: Princeton University Press, 1989), p. 4.

5. Pasteur Vallery-Radot, *Louis Pasteur: A Great Life in Brief,* trans. Alfred Joseph (New York: Alfred A. Knopf, 1970), p. 92.

6. Gerald L. Geison, *The Private Science of Louis Pasteur* (Princeton, N.J.: Princeton University Press, 1995), p. 30.

Chapter 9

1. Pasteur Vallery-Radot, *Louis Pasteur: A Great Life in Brief,* trans. Alfred Joseph (New York: Alfred A. Knopf, 1970), p. 128.

2. René Dubos, *Pasteur and Modern Science,* ed. Thomas D. Brock (Madison, Wis.: Science Tech, 1988), p. 90.

Chapter 10

1. Bruno Latour, *The Pasteurization of France,* trans. Alan Sheridan and John Law (Cambridge, Mass.: Harvard University Press, 1988), pp. 69–70.

2. René Dubos, *Pasteur and Modern Science,* ed. Thomas D. Brock (Madison, Wis.: Science Tech, 1988), p. 111.

3. René Dubos, *Louis Pasteur: Free Lance of Science* (New York: Da Capo, 1960), p. 339.

4. Ibid., pp. 339–340.

5. Pasteur Vallery-Radot, *Louis Pasteur: A Great Life in Brief,* trans. Alfred Joseph (New York: Alfred A. Knopf, 1970), p. 150.

Chapter 11

1. Eugene Linden, "Beware of Rabies," *Time*, August 23, 1993, pp. 58–59.

2. "Last Remaining Smallpox Virus Stocks to Be Destroyed on 30 June 1999," World Health Organization, May 25, 1996. (On the Internet at http://www.who.ch)

Chapter 12

1. Gerald L. Geison, *The Private Science of Louis Pasteur* (Princeton, N.J.: Princeton University Press, 1995), p. 261.

2. For more information on the Pasteur Institute, write: Institut Pasteur, 25 rue du Docteur Roux, 75724 Paris Cedex 15, France.

3. *Institut Pasteur: Towards a New Century* (Paris: Pasteur Institute, 1987), p. 35.

4. Geison, p. 262.

Chapter 13

1. René Dubos, *Louis Pasteur: Free Lance of Science* (New York: Da Capo, 1960), p. xxviii.

2. Pasteur Vallery-Radot, *Louis Pasteur: A Great Life in Brief,* trans. Alfred Joseph (New York: Alfred A. Knopf, 1970), p. 193.

3. Dubos, p. 57.

4. Pasteur Vallery-Radot, p. 197.

5. Dubos, p. 336.

6. Letter from Annick Perrot, Museum Curator, Pasteur Institute, November 22, 1996.

7. *The Story of Louis Pasteur*, directed by William Dieterle (1936). This movie is available on videotape.

Glossary

anaerobic bacteria—Bacteria that are active only when no oxygen is present.

anthrax—A disease that infects cattle and sheep and can be spread to humans.

antibiotic drug—A drug that works against a disease caused by bacteria or certain other microorganisms.

bacteria—Microorganisms of a certain type. Some bacteria cause disease, but others do not.

crystal—One of the regularly shaped objects that many substances form when they harden.

culture—A colony of microorganisms grown in a special substance for scientific study.

fermentation—A gradual chemical change in which sugar is changed into alcohol and carbon dioxide gas.

germ—A microbe.

germ theory—The theory that states that fermentation and certain diseases are caused by specific microorganisms.

infectious disease—A disease caused by a microbe. Many infectious diseases can be spread from human to human.

microbe—A microorganism that can cause disease.

microbiology—The branch of science that deals with microorganisms.

microorganism—A simple living thing, too small to be seen without a microscope. Some microorganisms cause disease, but others do not.

optical activity—The property of a substance that bends a beam of light that passes through it.

pasteurization—A process for heating milk or other liquids hot enough and long enough to kill harmful bacteria.

rabies—A deadly disease that people can get from the bite of an infected animal.

silkworm—A moth larva that spins threads of silk to make a cocoon.

smallpox—A serious disease that causes skin sores. Smallpox has been wiped out by vaccination.

spontaneous generation—The theory, now disproven, that living things arise from nonliving matter.

stereochemistry—The branch of science that deals with the position in space of tiny particles called atoms and how this affects such things as optical activity.

sterilization—The act of making something free of microorganisms.

theory—An explanation based on observation and reasoning.

vaccination—The giving of a preparation of weakened or killed microbes to a person or animal to prevent a disease.

yeast—A particular microorganism that grows quickly in the presence of sugar.

Further Reading

De Kruif, Paul. *Microbe Hunters*. San Diego, Calif.: Harcourt Brace, 1954.

Facklam, Howard, and Margery Facklam. *Bacteria*. New York: Henry Holt, 1994.

Silverstein, Alvin, Virginia Silverstein, and Robert Silverstein. *Rabies*. Springfield, N.J.: Enslow, 1994.

Symes, R. F., and R.R. Harding. *Crystal & Gem*. New York: Alfred A. Knopf, 1991.

Whaley, Paul. *Butterfly & Moth*. New York: Alfred A. Knopf, 1988.

Index